PARLIMENTARY IN REVIEW

A Hobar Publications Workbook

First Globe Pequot edition 2019

Published by Hobar Publications
An imprint of Globe Pequot Press
Wholly Owned by: The Rowman & Littlefield Publishing Group, Inc.
4501 Forbes Boulevard, Suite 200
Lanham, Maryland 20706

Distributed by National Book Network
1-800-462-6420

TABLE OF CONTENTS

Parliamentary in Review

Forward

Parliamentary in Review is a video tape designed to assist in the instruction of parliamentary procedure at any grade level or with any type of organization. The tape includes sevens lessons on parliamentary procedure plus a final lesson called the "Exciting 5 Minutes" which incorporates many of the parliamentary procedure rules learned in the previous lessons. The purpose of the "Exciting 5 Minutes" is three fold:

    (1)   to illustrate to the learner how parliamentary rules may be used.

    (2)   that using proper parliamentary procedure can expedite the conduct of meetings

    (3)   that parliamentary procedure can be fun

How to Use Enclosed Materials

This document has four separate parts. They are:

    (1)   a lesson plan outline (white sheet)

    (2)   table of parliamentary motions (green sheet)

    (3)   table showing object and effect of motions (blue sheet)

    (4)   a sheet of parliamentary terms (yellow sheet)

You will note that each lesson consists of the item of business, motions (rules) demonstrated, explanation of each motion (rule), and its object and effect. The lessons have been published in the same order as found on the video tape.

Order of Precedence (Priority)

Just a word on using the "table of Parliamentary Rules". As you observe this green sheet, you will note that the parliamentary motions are categorized into five groups. They are: privileged, incidental, subsidiary, principal, and unclassified motions.

Except for the unclassified motions these motions are listed in descending order of precedence or priority. A motion with a higher order of precedence means that it can be made while a motion of a lower precedence (priority) is on the floor. For example the main motion has the lowest priority; thus, any other motion can be made while is pending before the assembly. Generally speaking an incidental motion (since they have a higher precedence) can be made when a subsidiary motion is pending. Furthermore a privileged motion can be made when incidental or subsidiary motions are pending. Both the privileged and subsidiary motions have an order of precedence within themselves. Thus, in the privileged motions, adjourn has a higher priority than recess and recess has a higher priority than question of privilege. To fix the time to which to adjourn has the highest precedence of the privileged motions and thus can be made even after adjournment has been moved, seconded, and affirmatively voted upon. Within the subsidiary motions, to lay on the table has the highest precedence and thus can be made when any one of the other subsidiary motions is pending. There is no order of precedence within the incidental motions.

Method of Voting

There are five methods of voting: voice, hand, standing, ballot, and roll call. A division of the house, which is a standing vote, can be called only on a voice or hand vote. A member can move the method of voting anytime before the vote and anytime after the vote had been taken but not after another question (motion) has been stated.

Use of the Gavel

Two tapes of the gavel call the meeting to order while one tap is used to close the meeting. One tape of the gavel should be used after announcing the results of the vote on a motion. Some organizations may use three taps of the gavel to signal their members to rise and one tape of the gavel to signal them to sit.

I. INTRODUCTION

Parliamentary in Review is organized to assist the teacher to teach parliamentary procedure in an orderly and logical manner. This unit is developed so that the teacher may need only a limited amount of time to prepare for teaching this parliamentary procedure unit.

A. <u>Conduct of Meetings</u>

Robert's Rules prescribes a certain order in which business is conducted at most regular business meetings. The order with some statements of clarification follows:(See Transparency #1)

1. <u>Call Meeting to Order</u>

   * Two taps of gavel brings meeting to order.

   * Chair should state "I bring/call this meeting to order" -- NOT I <u>think</u> I'd like to bring this meeting to order.

2. <u>Reading of the Minutes</u>

   * There is no need to have a formal motion to approve/accept the minutes.

   * Chair asks for corrections after minutes are read.

   * If there are no corrections or when corrections have been completed, Chair will state "minutes are accepted as read or minutes are approved as corrected."

3. <u>Treasurer's Report</u>

   * Same as #2 above...

4. Standing Committee Reports

   *   Don't move to accept the committee report. Instead, move to accept recommendations...made by the committee, if appropriate.

   *   If no action is necessary on a committee report, the chair should thank the person making the report and go on to the next item of business.

5. Special Committee Reports

   *   This is a single purpose committee which dissolves once their task is completed (i.e. - Spring Picnic Committee).

   *   Use the same rules of reporting and handling these reports as stated in #4 above.

6. Unfinished business
   This may include...

   *   Postpone motions
   *   Tabled motions

   *   Motion to be reconsidered or rescinded

   *   Pending or unfinished agenda items from last meeting

7. New Business

   Any item of business not previously brought up at another meeting.

8. Announcement, program and adjournment

   *   Some organizations may make announcements, adjourn the business meeting and then have the program.

   *   It is also permissive to have the program before adjournment.

B. ORDER OF PRECEDENCE

Order of precedence or priority means that a motion can be made when a motion of a lower precedence or priority is on the floor.

The table of motions listed in the rear of this document shows 5 major categories of motions, as follows:

1. Principal Motion

    *   There is only one principal motion, that is the main motion -- the only motion which presents an item of business before the assembly.

    *   Should be made prior to debate (this rule is frequently violated in many organizations).

    *   Making the main motion prior to debate helps to keep debate focused on one subject.

    *   Is out of order if another main motion or any other motion is on the floor; thus, has the lowest precedence or priority of any motion.

2. Subsidiary Motion

    *   As the term applies, they are subsidiary to the main motion and somehow has an impact on its modification (i.e. - amendment), or distribution (i.e. - refer to committee or postpone).

    *   All subsidiary motions are of higher priority than the principal (main) motion.

    *   The subsidiary motions have an order of priority within themselves. To take from the table has the highest precedence or priority and to postpone indefinitely has the lowest priority within the subsidiary motion.

    *   Thus, to refer to a committee has a higher precedence than to amend; therefore, can be

4

made when a main motion and its amendment are pending.

3.   Incidental Motions

   *   These motions are incidental to the main motion.   They deal more with meeting procedures and not substance of a main motion.

   *   Usually incidentals have priority over subsidiary and main motions.

   *   Incidental motions have no particular priority within themselves.

4.   Privileged Motions

   *   These motions have priority over Incidental, Subsidiary and Main Motions.

   *   Except for adjournment, all privileged motions become Incidental Main Motions if there is no motion pending before the assembly when they are made.

   *   Adjournment is always a Privileged Motion except:

      1)   It is moved when the next meeting date has not been set so you are adjourning sine die (without a day for the next meeting);

      2)   When adjournment is qualified (i.e. - I move to adjourn at 8 p.m. which says when you want to adjourn and thus it qualifies adjournment).

5.   Unclassified Motion

   *   These motions don't fall into any of the other
       four categories.

   *   They may be moved when it is appropriate.

C.   **STEPS IN HANDLING A MOTION**

There are six steps that are necessary to handle a Main Motion. These are
as follows (see Transparency #2):

1)   Making the Motion - The procedure could look something like
     this:

     *   Member rises and states - "Mr. President"

     *   The president states - "The Chair recognizes
         Sue"

     *   Sue states - "I move we purchase jackets for
         our officers"

2)   Second

     *   Person can call second without being
         recognized

     *   In large meetings, it is sometimes required to
         give your name when you second the motion,
         and thus is so recorded by the secretary.

3)   Chair States the Question
     (i.e. - motion has been moved and seconded that we have a
     Spring picnic)

     *   Up to this point, the motion belongs to the
         proposer. After chair states motion, it belongs
         to the assembly.

4) <u>Debate</u>

* Each member may debate each debatable motion twice for 10 minutes each time (one exception is the debatable appeal)

* Rules as to whom the chair selects to debate if more than one member rises at one time to debate a motion are:

a) Proposer of the motion has the right to speak first. She cannot debate against her motion, but she doesn't have to debate it at all if she so desires. She may vote against her motion.

b) If none of the members rising to debate are the proposer of the motion, then call on the person who hasn't debated up to that time.

c) If the members rising to debate don't include the proposer and none of them have debated yet, select the one first who expresses a view not yet expressed (i.e. - if 2 members have risen previously to speak for the motion and of the 3 members now rising to debate 2 are for the motion and 1 against, you should call on the person against the motion first).

5. <u>Chair Puts the Question</u>

The Chair merely states - "all in favor of the motion that we . .. say Aye, opposed say No."

6. Vote

    *   Notice the number of Ayes and Noes.

    *   After the vote the chair should state the result -" The ayes (Noes) have it, the motion passes (fails) and the effect; We will (will not) purchase jackets for our officers."

D. **Methods of Voting**

There are Five methods of voting. They are 1) Hand, 2) Voice, 3) Standing, 4) Ballot, and 5) Roll Call Vote. A few facts regarding voting are:

    *   A division of the house (incidental motion #2 -See Table of Parliamentary Motion) may be called after a voice and hand vote. If called the chair must take a revote by standing.

    *   A chair/president must vote with the members on a ballot vote.

    *   As a rule a chair will not vote on a voice, hand, or standing vote unless the vote will effect the outcome. (ie. a tie vote on the motion to lay on the table the president/chair should not vote if he wants it to fail, however the president/chair should vote in the affirmative if he wants it to pass.

    *   On a roll call vote the secretary (clerk) will read all names of members alphabetical with the president or chair called last. The responses should be yes (in favor), no (opposed), present (abstain), or not ready to vote (pass). Votes can change up to the time it is announced by the president/chair. Note: The chair/president announces the vote not the clerk/secretary.

E. **Use of the Gavel**

The gavel should be used by the chair to exert authority and provide distinction and clarity to certain action such as:
    1) Opening the meeting - 2 taps
    2) After announcing votes on motions - 1 tap
    3) Adjourning the meeting - 1 tap

II LESSON PLANS
Lesson Outline

Lesson #	Item of Business	Abilities to be demonstrated	Requirements	Object & Effect
1A	*The club to purchase a trophy case for the school.	*Main motion *Amend *Informal question	G-D1 G-C7	B-27 B-25
1B	*The club to attend the state conference in June.	*Main motion *Request for information *Parliamentary inquiry *Refer to committee *Adjourn	G-D1 G-B12 G-B13 G-C5 G-A2	B-27 B-17 B-18 B-23 B-2
2A	*To sponsor a benefit dance for the food drive.	*Postpone to a certain time *Limit or extend time for debate *Raise a point of order *Division of the house	G-C4 G-C3 G-B3 G-B2	B-22 B-21 B-8 B-7
2B	*The club to visit the amusement park and purchase a camera.	*Divide a motion *Discussion *Take a recess *Discussion *Lay on the table	G-B5 G-A3 G-C1	B-10 B-3 B-19
3A	*To ratify the officers decision: to purchase flowers for our advisor who is ill.	*Ratify	G-E5	B-32
3B	*To take from the table the club to purchase a camera.	*Take from the table *Amend *Amend an amendment *Informal question *Call for the previous question (all motions pending)	G-E1 G-C7 G-C6 G-C2	B-28 B-25 B-24 B-20
4A	*To rescind the club purchasing a trophy case for the school.	*Rescind-previous notice given *Question of privilege *Appeal a decision of the chair.	G-E4 G-A4 G-B1	B-31 B-4 B-6
4B	*The club to sell raffle tickets for a fund raiser.	*To modify or withdraw a motion	G-B6	B-11
5A	*To reconsider that the club visit the amusement park.	*Reconsider *To fix the time to which to adjourn *Call for the orders of the day	G-E2 G-A1 G-A5	B-29 B-1 B-5
5B	*To support our advisor's nomination for the school board.	*Object to the consideration of the question	*G-B4	B-9
6A	*The club to hold our next month's meeting on the 3rd Tuesday of the month.	*Suspend the rules	G-B8	B-13

6B	*To reopen nominations for the office of president.	*Reopen nominations *Nominate *Close nominations *Method of voting	G-B10 G-B7 G-B9 G-B11	B-15 B-12 B-14 B-16
7	*The chapter officers to buy pizza for the entire membership.	*Parliamentary procedure		
8	*Mock contest(Wisconsin Future Farmers of America Parliamentary Contest Rules applied)			

G-Green Sheet
B-Blue Sheet

II. Lesson Plans

Each lesson will include the following: 1) parliamentary ability to be stated, 2) key points to be considered and 3) study (test) question on those two lessons (i.e. 1A and 1B).

Lesson #1

1. **Key Points**

    A. Main Motion

        *   Should be made to introduce an item of business

        *   Proper wording is "I move that . . ." - "I so move" and "I make a motion" are incorrect

        *   Should be made prior to debate on the item of business.

    B. Amend

        *   Three ways to amend are: 1) add, 2) strike out, and 3) both add and strike out.

        *   Can only be one primary amendment and one secondary amendment(amendment to the amendment) to the main motion pending at any given time.

    C. Request for Information

        *   Information dealing with non parliamentary items.

        *   Can interrupt speaker.

        *   Proper wording - "Mr. Chairman, I rise to a point of information."

    D. Parliamentary Inquiry

        *   Questions dealing only with parliamentary procedure.

        *   May be used instead of point of order if you are not sure that the person is out of order.

11

*   A "kinder" way of correcting a person who is out of order.

*   Proper wording is "Mr. Chairman I rise to a Parliamentary Inquiry."

E.   Refer to Committee

*   Person making the motion to refer is usually appointed to the committee (unless referred to a standing committee) and is the chairman of the committee.

*   Proper wording is "I refer to a committee of three, appointed by the chair, the motion that . . ." or "I move to refer to the finance committee the motion that . . ."

F.   Adjourn

*   Can be made while other motions are pending.
*   Meeting is not adjourned until the chairman says so.

*   After the motion to adjourn passes the chairman should hesitate prior to declaring the meeting adjourned.

*   Things which can occur after the motion to adjourn passes and before the chairman declared adjournment are: 1) motion made to fix the time to which to adjourn, 2) move to reconsider, 3) move to reconsider and enter on the minutes, and 4) announcements.

2. **Questions for Lesson #1**

A.   What is the only motion which introduces an item of business before the assembly?

B.   What are the three ways a motion can be amended?

C. What is the difference between the motion to rise to parliamentary inquiry and request for information?

D. When a motion is referred to an ad hoc or special committee (not a standing committee), who is the person usually appointed as chairman?

E. What four things can occur after the motion to adjourn has passed and prior to the chairman declaring the meeting adjourned?

NOTE: See answers to questions in the back of this document.

LESSON #2

1. **Key Points to Consider**

   A. Postpone to a Certain Time

   * A motion can be postpone to later in the meeting or to the next meeting providing the group meets at least every three months.

   * If the motion is postponed until the next meeting it is taken up with "unfinished business" at the next meeting.

   * Proper wording is: " I move to postpone to our next meeting the motion that . . . "

   B. Limit or Extend Time for Debate

   * Can limit or extend number of debate per member or length of time of each debate.

   * Motion needs a two-thirds vote.

   * Proper wording is "I move to limit debate to one debate per member."

   C. Raise a Point of Order

   * Used to correct a member who is out of order (i.e. irrelevant debate or making a motion with a lower precedence then the pending motion).

13

*   Proper wording is: " Madame Chairman I rise to a point of order"

*   Can interrupt a speaker.

D.   <u>Division of the House(Assembly)</u>

*   Called by a member who desires a revote.

*   Can be "demanded" by one member, no second is needed

*   Revote usually is a standing vote

E.   <u>Divide a Motion</u>

*   Can be moved by a member if the parts of the original motion are different and can stand by themselves (see item of business Lesson 2B)

*   If parts of the motions are not related (i.e. moving to accept a group of unrelated resolutions) then the one member can request to divide the question (no second is required) without the need for a vote.

*   Proper wording is "I move to divide the motion with the first part being ....and the second part being ...."

F.   <u>Take a Recess</u>

*   Can be amended as to length of time.

*   After the recess the meeting must be brought back to order (two taps of the gavel) and business continues where you left off prior to recess.

*   Proper wording is: " I move we take a fifteen minute recess."

G.   To Lay on the Table

*   Purpose of tabling a motion is to delay action but not to kill the motion. If you want to kill a motion use the motion to postpone indefinitely.

*   Must be removed from the table this meeting or next which must be held during the next 3 months after the motion was tabled. Thus a motion can't be tabled at an annual meeting when it is the last item of business at that meeting.

2. **Questions for Lesson #2**

T F A.   A motion can be postponed for up to 6 meetings.

T F B.   To take a recess is always an incidental motion.

T F C.   Any member can raise a point of order.

T F D.   A motion which includes different subjects can be divided on the request of one member. This request doesn't require a second or a vote.

T F E.   The purpose of tabling a motion is to kill it.

LESSON #3

1. **Key Points to Consider**

A.   To Ratify

*   Ratification approve/disapprove actions taken by a committee or executive board.

B.   Take From the Table

*   See to table Lesson #2 F.

*   Usually handled during the unfinished business of the next meeting or during a lull period of the

present meeting. Must be at least one item of business conducted between the time the motion was tabled and taken from the table.

C.   Amend

*   See Lesson #1 B.

D.   Amend the Amendment

*   This motion amends the amendment and not the main motion.

*   Can only be one such motion pending at one time on the main motion.

*   Is voted upon prior to voting on the amendment.

*   Whereas an amendment is called an amendment of the "1st order" or "primary amendment." This motion is called an "amendment of the second order" or a "secondary amendment."

E.   Informal Questions

*   Handle as a request (i.e. The chairman states the question has been informally called. Are you ready to vote?). If there is one dissenter the motion is not voted upon.

*   This request can be made without being recognized by the chair. (i.e. During a lull in the debate a member can just call out "Question".)

F.   Call for the Previous Question

*   Formal motion to close debate.

*   If more than one motion is pending (i.e. a motion and its amendment) the motion to move the previous question, if passed, closed debate

only on the most recently moved motion (in this case, the amendment).

* If you wish to close debate on all motions the motion is "I move the previous question on all pending questions" or "I move the previous question on the main motion and its amendments."

2. Questions for Lesson #3

T F A. Ratification is used to approve actions taken by a committee or executive board.

T F B. A motion to take from the table has priority over the motion to postpone.

T F C. You may have more than one primary amendment to a motion pending at a time.

T F D. When a member informally calls "question" the chairman is required to immediately proceed to the vote on the pending motion.

T F E. The motion to call for the previous question received 10 votes in favor and 8 votes opposed. You therefore proceed to vote on the pending question.

Lesson #4

1. Key Points to Consider

A. To Rescind

* If previous notice has been given at the last meeting or in the call of the meeting (i.e. meeting announcement) than a two-thirds vote is not necessary for adoption of the motion.

* Two forms of recision are:

1. To annul

2. To amend something previously adopted.

* Motion to rescind is not in order if part or all of the action to rescind has been carried out.

B. Question of Privilege

* Can interrupt a speaker.

* Is a privileged motion only when an item of business is pending when a question of privilege is raised.

* Proper wording is "Madame Chairman I rise to a question of privilege affecting the assembly." (Note: a member does not need to be recognized prior to indicating the reason he rose to speak.)

* The members request is usually handled by the chair without a vote.

C. Appeal the Decision of the Chair

* Purpose is to reverse the chairs decision.

* Motion is put in the affirmative (i.e. "all those in favor of the chairs decision that . . . . say aye. Opposed say no.") Thus to reverse the chairs decision you need more no votes than aye votes.

* If the appeal is debatable each member can debate only once whereas the chairman can debate twice.

* If appeal is undebatable the chairman may give her reasons for the decision she made.

D. To Modify or Withdraw a Motion

* Can only be initiated by the person who moved the motion to be withdrawn or modified.

* The request to withdraw needs unanimous consent (i.e. the chair states "a request has

been made to withdraw the motion. Is there any objection?" short pause -"Seeing none the motion is withdrawn.")

* If the request is denied than any member can move to withdraw the motion. This motion requires a majority vote to pass. It also requires a second if this motion is made by the member who had moved the motion which is being withdrawn or modified.

2. **Questions for Lesson #4**

T F A. The purposes of the motion to rescind is to annul or amend a motion previously adopted.

T F B. A member can't rise to a question of privilege when another member is debating a motion.

T F C. A vote on the appeal of the chair's decision resulted in a vote of 14 ayes and 20 noes. Thus the appeal failed.

T F D. A debatable appeal can only be debated once by each member.

T F E. Any member can moves to withdraw or modify a motion at anytime during debate.

Lesson #5

Key Points to Consider

A. Reconsider

* This motion to reconsider must be made on the same day or next calendar day of which the motion to be reconsidered was made.

* A member moving to reconsider must have been on the prevailing side of the vote on the motion which is to be reconsidered. i.e. If a

motion to purchase a movie camera failed and a member wants to reconsider that motion he must have voted with the "no" vote on the motion mentioned above.

* A motion to reconsider may be made and seconded but not taking up until later if other items of business are pending. It may be called up later by the member who moved the motion to reconsider when there is an "opening on the agenda" in the meeting.

B. <u>To Fix the Time to Which to Adjourn</u>

* Purpose of this motion is to set the time for the next meeting.

* If made when no other business is pending it becomes an incidental main motion.

* Can be made even after the motion to adjourn has been voted upon.

C. <u>Call for the Orders of the Day</u>

* Orders of the day is the meeting agenda.

* A call for the orders alerts the chairman that she needs to proceed with the next item (schedule) of business.

D. <u>Objection to Consideration of the Question</u>

* Needs a two-thirds vote against consideration for objection to pass

* Motion is stated "all those in favor of considering the question that..."

2. **Questions for Lesson #5**

T F A. A member can move to reconsider a motion passed at last months' meeting.

T F B. Any member can move to reconsider a motion.

T F   C.   The motion to reconsider is amendable.

T F   D.   The motion to fix the time to which to adjourn sets the time for the next meeting of that group or organization.

T F   E.   The motion to fix the time to which to adjourn can be made after the vote to adjourn has passed.

Lesson #6

1. Key Points to Consider

A.   Suspend the Rules

*   Can suspend parliamentary (two-thirds vote) and standing rules (simple majority vote) but not constitutional or bylaws rules unless a provision in the bylaws state that it is possible to suspend that specific rule.

*   Rule that is suspended is done so for only that particular time and the rule goes back into effect after that time.

B.   Reopen Nominations

*   Usually done due to the lack of nominees.

*   Usually done for a specified amount of time.

C.   To Nominate

*   Does not need a second.

*   A member can immediately refuse the nomination if she so desires.

D.   Close Nominations

*   Chair may close nominations without a vote if he sees that there are no further nominations.

* A member wanting to nominate someone takes priority to a motion to close nominations.

E. Method of Voting

* See section on voting discussed earlier in this document.

* Method of voting can be decided by vote, unanimous consent, standing rules, or bylaw rules.

* On a ballot vote, when the ballots are being counted the business meeting may continue and the results of the ballot vote can be announced later providing the results of the ballot vote has no impact on the next item(s) of business.

2. Questions of Lesson 6

T F A. A reason for reopening nominations is to obtain more nominees.

T F B. The motion to nominate needs a second.

T F C. The motion to close nominations requires a two-thirds vote.

T F D. If there is only one candidate to be voted upon a member can move to accept this nominee by casting a unanimous ballot (vote) for the nominee.

T F E. A member may move the method of voting to be by ballot.

T F F. To suspend a parliamentary rule you need a two-thirds vote in favor of doing so.

T F G. Usually a rule in the by-laws can not be suspended

Answers To Quiz Questions

1. **Lesson One**

   A. Main Motion.

   B. Add, strike out, and both.

   C. Parliamentary inquiry deals with parliamentary procedure whereas request for information deals with parliamentary information.

   D. The person making the referral.

   E. Announcements, move to reconsider, move to reconsider and enter on the minutes, and move to fix the time to which to adjourn.

2. **Lesson Two**

   A. False. Only later in this meeting or the next if the groups meets at least every three months.

   B. False. Recess is a privileged motion if made when a pending item of business is on the floor. Otherwise it is an incidental main motion.

   C. True. Even the chairman can call a member out of order. Members rising to point of order must direct their point of orders to the chairman.

   D. True. That is correct.

   E. False. The motion to table should only delay action on a motion while other more urgent business is being conducted.

3. **Lesson Three**

   A. True. That is correct if the motion to ratify passes.

   B. True. That is correct.(See table of parliamentary motions in the back of this document.)

C. False. Only one amendment to a motion (primary amendment) can be pending at a time.

D. False. The chair should state "The question has been informally called are there any objections" (or are you ready to vote) if one member objects (since you need unanimous consent to proceed to the vote) you continue with the debate.

E. False. Previous question needs a two-thirds vote which in this case didn't occur.

4. Lesson Four

A. True.

B. False. A member can interrupt a speaker since the privilege may have to be carried out prior to the speaker terminating her debate i.e. a member rises to a question of privilege indicates she can't hear the speaker because the microphone has not been turned on.

C. False. The appeal passed and the Chairs decision is reversed. Remember the chair states this motion in the affirmative that is she must state "all those in favor of the chairs decision say aye - opposed say no." Since there were more no votes the chairs decision is reversed.

D. True. This is the one exception to the two debate rule mentioned earlier under rules of debate. The chair, however, can debate twice.

E. False. Only the person who made the main motion which is to be modified or withdrawn can indicate an effort to have her action withdrawn or modified. If she requests to do so and one member objects than any member can formally move to withdraw or modify.

5. Lesson Five

A. False. See discussion in lesson five.

B. False. Only the member who was on the prevailing side of the vote on the original main motion can move to reconsider.

C. False.

D. True. This motion has nothing to do with setting the time to adjourn the present meeting.

E. True. The motion to fix the time to which adjourned can be made after the vote on adjournment has been passed.

6. Lesson Six

A. True. This is probably the most frequent reason for doing so.

B. False. In most societies and organizations this is not true. You will see members who are not familiar with Robert Rules of Order frequently doing this incorrectly since they feel all nominations made from the floor need a second.

C. True. However the Chair can declare nominations closed if there are no other nominations being made.

D. False. Robert states that the motion is out of order since no one can vote for you. i.e. Suppose that such a motion is allowed and the vote is 22 - 5. Is this a unanimous vote? The answer is obviously no. At political conventions you see members casting unanimous ballots however these are rules adapted by their conventions and then they are superseding parliamentary rules.

E. True. This is true unless there are rules in the bylaws which states that the voting needs to be by another method. i.e. Roll Call

F. True. Whereas simple standing rules need only a majority vote to pass.

G. True. Unless there is a provision in the bylaws to do so. If so, a two-thirds vote would be needed to suspend the rule.

ORDER OF BUSINESS
REGULAR MEETING

Meeting Called To Order

Reading Of The Minutes

Report Of The Treasurer

Standing Committee Reports

Special Committee Reports

Unfinished Business

New Business

Announcements

Program

Adjournment

SIX STEPS IN HANDLING A MOTION

1. Making the motion

2. Second

3. Chair states the question

4. Debate

5. Chair puts the question

6. Vote

REVISED RULES (September 1999) – Table of Parliamentary Procedure Motions *

MOTIONS	Need a Second	Amend-able	Debatable	Vote Req'd	Interrupt Speaker	Reconsider
A. Privileged Motions 1. To fix the time to which to adjourn (1)	Yes	(4)	No	Majority	No	Yes
2. Adjourn (2)	Yes	No	No	Majority	No	No
3. Take a recess (3)	Yes	(4)	No	Majority	No	No
4. Raise a question of privilege	No	No	No	Decision of Chair (5)	Yes	No
5. Call for the orders of the day	No	No	No	Handled by Chair (6)	Yes	No
B. Incidental Motions 1. To appeal a decision of the chair	Yes	No	Yes (9)	Majority	Yes (24)	Yes
2. To call for a division of the house	No	No	No	Standing Vote (11)	Yes	No
3. To raise a point of order	No	No	No	Decision of Chair (8)	Yes	No
4. To object to consideration of a question	No	No	No	2/3	No (25)	(15)
5. To divide a motion or call for consideration by parts (10)	Yes	Yes	No	Majority	No (22)	No
6. To modify or withdraw a motion	No	No	No	Majority of (21) Unan. Consent	No	No
7. To nominate	No	(12)	(12)	(12)	No	No
8. To suspend the rules (14)	Yes	No	No	2/3 (20)	No	No
9. Close nominations	Yes	Yes	No	2/3	No	No
10. Reopen nominations	Yes	Yes	No	Majority	No	(15)
11. Method of voting	Yes	Yes	No	Majority	No	No
12. Request for information	No	No	No	No	Yes	No
13. Parliamentary inquiry	No	No	No	No	Yes	No
C. Subsidiary Motions 1. To lay on the table	Yes	No	No	Majority	No	No
2. To call for the previous question	Yes	No	No	2/3	No	(19)
3. To limit or extend time for debate	Yes	Yes	No	2/3	No	Yes
4. To postpone to a certain time	Yes	Yes	Yes	Majority	No	Yes
5. To refer to a committee	Yes	Yes	Yes	Majority	No	Yes (26)
6. To amend and amendment	Yes	No	Yes	Majority	No	Yes
7. To amend or substitute	Yes	Yes	Yes (7)	Majority	No	Yes
8. To postpone indefinitely	Yes	No	Yes	Majority	No	(18)
D. Principal Motion 1. A main motion	Yes	Yes	Yes	Majority	No	Yes
E. Unclassified 1. Take from the table	Yes	No	No	Majority	No	No
2. Reconsider	Yes	No	(13)	Majority	No (23)	No
3. Reconsider and enter on the minutes	Yes	Must be	called	up at next	meeting	(16)
4. Rescind	Yes	Yes	Yes	(17)	No (23)	(15)
5. Ratify	Yes	Yes	Yes	Majority	No	(15)

* Refer to Notes Pertaining to Specific Treatment of Motions on back of page.

NOTES PERTAINING TO SPECIFIC TREATMENT OF MOTIONS

1. Is a privileged motion only if made while another motion is pending, and in an assembly that made no provision for meeting on the same or next day; otherwise it is a main motion. The answers apply to the privileged motion.
2. When unqualified, is always a privileged motion except when effect would be to disband the group permanently. The answers apply to the privileged motion, not to a main motion to adjourn.
3. Is a privileged motion if made when other business is pending, otherwise is a main motion. Answers apply to the privileged motion.
4. Can be amended as to time.
5. Is usually disposed by chair, without vote.
6. Chair should proceed to order of the day or put a question as to whether the group wishes to proceed with the order. A motion not to proceed to order requires a 2/3 vote, the same as suspending the rules.
7. Can be debated only when the question being amended is debatable.
8. Is usually decided by chair, without calling for a vote.
9. Cannot be debatable if made during a division of the assembly, or when the pending question is undebatable. Cannot be debated when it apples to indecorum, transgression of the rules of speaking, or to priority of business.
10. The question must be divided at the request of a single member, (this request can be made when another has the floor), provided the resolutions relate to different subjects and are independent of each other.
11. When a division is called for, the chair proceeds to take the vote again by rising. No vote is taken on whether a division shall be made, i.e., on whether a standing vote shall be taken.
12. To nominate, one simply rises, addresses the presiding officer, and states, "I nominate _____ and is again seated.
13. Debatable when the question to be considered is debatable.
14. Applies only to standing rules or to rules of order; it may not be in conflict with the constitution or by-laws.
15. The motion can be reconsidered only if the prevailing vote was a negative one.
16. Outranks the motion to reconsider and can be made immediately after the other, providing a vote has not yet been taken on it.
17. The motion requires a 2/3's majority vote if notice of the motion to be proposed has not been given at the preceding meeting or in the call of the meeting.
18. Can be reconsidered only if vote was affirmative.
19. Must be moved before any vote has been taken on the motions upon which the previous question was moved.
20. Generally only applied to rules of parliamentary procedure. Simple standing rules require only a simple majority for their suggestion.
21. If a formal motion to withdraw or modify is made by the proposer of the original motion, it needs a second.
22. If a motion must be divided on the demand of one member, he/she can do so when another member has the floor and is speaking.
23. Motion to rescind can be made when another person has the floor, but cannot interrupt the speaker.
24. At the time of appealed ruling.
25. Objection to reconsideration of question can be made after another person has been assigned the floor and before he/she has spoken.
26. Up to the time the committee begins its work.

Revised 9/99

TABLE TO SHOW OBJECT AND EFFECT OF MOTIONS

	Kind of Motion	Object	Effect
1.	To fix the time to which to adjourn	To have legal continuation of the meeting	Sets definite continuation time
2.	To adjourn	End the meeting	Adjourns the meeting
3.	To take a recess	To secure an intermission	Delays action
4.	To raise a question of privilege	To correct undesirable condition	Corrects undesirable
5.	To call for the orders of the day	To secure adherence to order of business	Same as object
6.	To appeal a decision of the chair	To determine the attitude of the group on the ruling made by the chair	Secures ruling of the group rather than by the chair
7.	To call for a division	(a) to determine the accuracy of a voice vote (b) to secure expression individual member's voice	Secures an accurate check on vote
8.	To raise a point of order	To call attention to violation of rules	Keeps the organization functioning according to parliamentary procedure
9.	To object to the consideration of the question	Prevent wasting time on unimportant business	Suppress the motion
10.	To divide the question	Secure more careful consideration of parts	Secures action by parts
11.	To modify or withdraw	To change and eliminate	Motion is changed or eliminated allowing for a new motion
12.	To nominate	Suggest names for office	Places before the group names for consideration
13.	To suspend the rules	To permit action not possible under the rules	Secure action which otherwise would be prevented by rules

OBJECT AND EFFECT OF MOTIONS CONTINUED

	Kind of Motion	Object	Effect
14.	Close nominations	To finalize slate of candidates	Allows members to vote
15.	Reopen nominations	Attain new candidates	Introduces new candidates for office
16.	Method of voting	Determine type of vote	Select one of five methods of voting
17.	To make a request for information	To secure information or to be excused from a duty	Provide information
18.	Parliamentary inquiry	Obtain parliamentary information	Facilitates proper use of parliamentary rules
19.	To lay on the table	Clear the floor for more urgent business	Delays action
20.	To call for previous question	Secure immediate vote on pending question	Ends debate
21.	To limit or extend time for debate	Provides more or less time for discussion	Shortens or lengthens discussion period
22.	To postpone definitely (to a certain time)	Often gives more time for informal discussion and for securing followers	Delays action
23.	To commit or refer	To enable more careful consideration to be given	Delays action
24.	To amend the amendment	To improve the amendment	To change the amendment
25.	To amend	To improve the motion	To change the original motion
26.	To postpone indefinitely	To prevent a vote on the question	To suppress the question
27.	Main Motion	Introduce item of business to assembly	Proper method of handling business
28.	To take from the table	Continue the consideration of the question	Continue consideration of the question

OBJECT AND EFFECT OF MOTIONS CONTINUED

	Kind of Motion	Object	Effect
29.	To reconsider	To reconsider the question	Secures further consideration and another vote on question
30.	Reconsider and enter on minutes	Stops action on a motion	Can't consider until next day
31.	To rescind	Repeal action	Same as object
32.	To ratify	Approves a previous action taken	Same as object

PARLIAMENTARY TERMS

adhere	- attached to
adjourned meeting	- a meeting that is a legal continuation of a previous meeting, the meetings making up one session
adopt	- accept or agree to
agenda	- an outline of the order of business which is to come before the group that session
assembly	- the members of a society that have assembled for the transaction of business
ballot	- a secret vote, written on a slip of paper
by-laws	- fundamental rules or laws of an organization (also used to include constitution)
committee	- a group of members selected for specific duties
dilatory motion	- a frivolous or absurd motion used to delay action
ex officio	- a virtue of office (the president may be an ex officio member of certain committees)
general consent	- consent without a single objection (also called unanimous consent)
germane	- closely related to or having a direct bearing on the pending question
incidental motion	- is said to be incidental because it alters motions or matters which arise with few exceptions; incidental matters are related to the main question in such a way that they must be decided immediately before business can proceed
indecorum	- improper conduct or behavior
main motion	- a motion that brings business before the assembly
majority	- more than half
majority vote	- more than half of the votes cast
meeting	- a single official gathering to transact business

member	- an individual having the right of full participation in meetings (right to make motions, debate, and vote)
minutes	- the written report of the proceedings of the meeting
motion	- a formal proposal that certain action be taken
new business	- matters presented to the assembly for consideration that had not been carried over from previous meetings
parliamentary procedure	- rules used by an organization to conduct its meetings
pending question	- a motion that has been stated by the chair and is under consideration by the assembly
plurality vote	- largest number of voted given to any of the choices when three or more choices are possible
precedence	- order of priority of motions
prevailing side	- the winning side after a vote
previous notice	- announcement that a particular motion will be introduced at the meeting
privileged motion	- they do not relate to the pending business but have to do with special matters of immediate and overriding information which without debate should be allowed to interrupt the consideration of anything else
pro term	- temporary, for the time being
putting the question	- placing the motion before the assembly for a vote
question	- a motion
quorum	- the minimum number of members that must be present at a meeting for business to be legally transacted
roll call vote	- a vote taken by calling out the names of the members for the purpose of recording how each member votes
rules of order	- rules that relate to parliamentary procedure
session	- a meeting or series of connected meetings devoted to a single order of business
special committee	- a committee formed to perform a special function that will dissolve upon completion of its task (also called ad hoc committee)

standing committee	- permanent committee that performs continuing functions
standing rules	- rules that relate to details of administration rather than relating to parliamentary procedure
subsidiary motion	- assist the assembly in treating or disposing of a main motion; they are always applied to another motion and their adoption always does something to this motion; they can be applies to any main motion
unfinished business	- business carried over from the previous meeting
vote	- an expression of opinion or choice, either positive or negative, made by a member or group of members
yield	- concede to, give way to

www.ingramcontent.com/pod-product-compliance
Lightning Source LLC
Chambersburg PA
CBHW081749200326
41597CB00024B/4448